"WHAT IF YOU ARE A SUPERHERO AND YOU DON'T KNOW!"

"Awakening the Extraordinary Within You and Embracing Your Inner Gift"

Rishabh Agarwal

WHAT IF YOU ARE A SUPERHERO AND YOU DON'T KNOW!

Author : Rishabh Agarwal

ISBN : 978-93-88018-49-4

First Edition : 2025

Price : 275/-

© Author

All Rights reserved. No part of this work may be copied, reproduced, adopted, abridged or translated, stored in any retrieval system, computer system, photographic or other system transmitted in any from by any means whether electronic, mechanical, digital, photographic or otherwise, without a prior written permission of Author/publisher.

Published & Printed by :

First print Publications
Tagore Town, Prayagraj-211002
E-mail : firstprintpublications@gmail.com

DEDICATIONS

THIS BOOK IS FOR YOU.

To my Late father

*Shri N. K. Agarwal,
who left for his heavenly abode in 2024. It was his inspiration and guidance that shaped me into who I am today. His unwavering belief in my abilities continues to be the foundation of my journey.*

> TO ALL THE HIDDEN SUPERHEROES OF THE WORLD THOSE WHO CARRY UNTAPPED POTENTIAL WITHIN THEM, UNAWARE OF THE EXTRAORDINARY GIFTS THEY POSSESS.

Foreword

Have you ever felt that there's something special within you—something waiting to be discovered, nurtured, and shared with the world?

This book is a journey of self-discovery, inspired by the belief that every person carries a unique, God-gifted ability. Far too often, these abilities remain dormant, buried under the weight of routine, responsibilities, and societal expectations.

Together, we'll embark on a transformative journey, uncovering the superhero within you. This isn't just a book—it's your invitation to awaken your power, embrace your purpose, and leave the world better than you found it.

Let's begin.

Preface

What if You Are a Superhero and You Don't Know!

Have you ever felt like life has boxed you into a routine, leaving your dreams and potential on the sidelines? Maybe you've wondered, "Is this all there is to my story?" If so, you're not alone. Many of us live our lives unaware of the incredible power and unique gifts we possess.

This book is here to change that.

Imagine you're a superhero—not the kind who wears a cape or leaps tall buildings in a single bound (aka Spiderman), but someone with a unique gift, a strength that only you can bring to the world. You may not have realized it yet, but within you lies an extraordinary ability waiting to be discovered. It could be the gift of creativity, leadership, compassion, resilience, or something entirely unique.

When we hear the word superhero, our minds often jump to images of Spiderman leaping between skyscrapers, Superman soaring through the clouds while saving a plummeting airplane, Batman battling vicious villains in the dead of night, or Iron Man—a genius billionaire with a high-tech suit—fighting to save humanity. These extraordinary characters captivate us with their supernatural powers and larger-than-life abilities. But No. A big No. That's not the kind of superhero I'm here to talk about.

The superhero I'm referring to doesn't fly or wear a suit of armour. The superhero I see in you possesses gifts far greater than super strength or speed—gifts that have the power to change the world in ways you might not even realize.

Think about Pablo Picasso, who transformed the world of art with his unparalleled creativity. Or Paulo Coelho, who inspired millions with his words and wisdom as an author. Abraham Lincoln—who, through leadership, changed the course of history. Andrew Carnegie, the industrialist who reshaped economies and brought prosperity to nations. Warren Buffett, whose vision and strategic mind turned him into the most legendary investor the world has ever seen. Or even Chanakya, the ancient strategist and philosopher whose brilliance shaped entire empires.

None of these people had superhuman strength, the ability to fly, or high-tech gadgets. Yet, they discovered their true gift, unlocked their potential, and left a lasting legacy.

You see, being a superhero isn't about leaping tall buildings—it's about recognizing the unique qualities within you that can inspire change, create greatness, and leave the world better than you found it. Whether it's creativity, leadership, compassion, resilience, or something entirely unique, your gift—your superpower—is waiting to be uncovered.

This book is here to help you find it.

But why don't we see these gifts?

Because life happens. We get caught up in jobs, family responsibilities, and societal norms. The world often convinces us to fit in, to conform, and in the process, we forget to explore the vast potential within us.

This book is your roadmap to rediscovering that gift. Through stories, reflections, and actionable insights, we will:

- Help you identify your unique superpower.

- Break the barriers that hold you back.

- Show you how to harness your gift to make a difference.

By the time you finish this journey, my hope is that you'll see yourself in a whole new light—not as just another person in the crowd, but as a superhero with the power to impact your life and the world around you.

Because the truth is, the world needs your gift. It needs your light, your strength, and your unique perspective.

So, are you ready to step into your power?

Let's begin this incredible journey together.

— **Rishabh Agarwal**

Contents

Foreword   iv
Preface   v

1. The Gifts We Leave Behind   12
2. The Hidden Diamond Within You   18
3. Breaking Free From The Invisible Rope   24
4. The Fear Of Flying: Overcoming Self-Doubt   30
5. The Superhero Inside   36
6. Some Birds Aren't Meant To Be Caged   42
7. The Road Less Chosen   50
8. The Unseen Force Around You: Notice Your Energy   58
9. It's Never Too Late   64
10. The Danger Of Aiming Too Low   76
11. The Ripple Effect Of Your Superpower   82

12. Legacy: Leaving The World
    A Better Place   90
13. Conclusion: The World Needs Your
    Superpowers   97
14. Final Words of Inspiration   103

1

The Gifts We Leave Behind

# Chapter One

The Gifts We Leave Behind

"Within each of us lies dormant superpowers. Unleash them, and you'll find your true purpose."

Have you ever cleaned out an old drawer or stumbled upon a dusty box in the attic, only to discover something you'd forgotten you owned? Maybe it was an old photograph, a letter, or a childhood toy. In that moment, you felt a rush of nostalgia—a reminder of a part of you that had been set aside but never truly lost.

Now imagine that same scenario, but instead of a forgotten object, it's a part of yourself—a gift, a talent, or a dream you once had. What if life, in its endless busyness, caused you to tuck that gift away?

This chapter is about those forgotten treasures—the gifts we leavebehind.

The Early Spark

As children, we're naturally drawn to what excites us. A child who loves drawing might have the seeds of an artist within them. A child who enjoys solving puzzles may have a mind for strategy. But as we grow, these sparks often dim. We're told to focus on what's "practical" or "realistic." And so, we trade our passions for the expectations of others.

Think back to your own childhood. What lit you up? Was it writing stories, helping others, exploring nature, or creating something new? Those early sparks are clues to the gifts you've always carried.

The Drift Into Routine

Fast forward to adulthood. The demands of life—career, bills, responsibilities—begin to take center stage. It's not that we intentionally forget our gifts; we just get caught up in surviving, not thriving.

Here's the truth: your gifts didn't disappear. They're still there, waiting for you to notice them again.

The Story of Lord Hanuman

In the timeless tale from Ramayana, the story of young Lord Hanuman beautifully illustrates the concept of forgotten gifts.

As a child, Hanuman was full of life, confidence, and an extraordinary sense of curiosity. He was no ordinary child—he had immense power, gifted to him by divine forces. One day, as he played under the vast sky, he saw the sun shining brightly in the distance. Its fiery red hue reminded him of a luscious fruit. Believing it to be something he could eat, Hanuman leaped into the sky, soaring with confidence and determination toward the mighty sun.

Nothing could hold him back. Not the vastness of space, not the heat of the sun. His strength and belief in himself were limitless. The gods watched in awe as this child, full of courage and power, dared to approach the sun itself.

However, this act of boldness caused concern among the celestial beings. Fearing the consequences of Hanuman's unchecked powers, they placed a curse upon him. The curse didn't take away his abilities, but it clouded his memory of them. From that day forward, Hanuman's extraordinary gifts lay dormant, hidden from his own awareness.

It wasn't until much later, during the events of the Ramayana, that Hanuman was reminded of his divine powers by Jambavan, the wise king of the bears. When he was tasked with crossing the ocean to find Mata Sita, he hesitated, unsure of his ability to perform such a monumental task. It was only through the encouragement of Jambavan that he rediscovered the truth: he was capable of leaping across oceans, moving mountains, and accomplishing the impossible.

The Lesson: Find Your Jambavan

Hanuman's story is a powerful metaphor for our own lives. Like Hanuman, we are born with gifts—unique abilities that make us extraordinary. But as life unfolds, these gifts are often buried under doubt, fear, and routine. We forget our potential, much like Hanuman forgot his divine powers.

Yet, just as Hanuman rediscovered his strength when the moment called for it, so can we. Sometimes, it takes a reminder from someone who sees our potential, much like Jambavan did for Hanuman. Other times, it's about quieting the noise of life and looking within.

The lesson is clear: Surround yourself with those who encourage and uplift you, those who believe in your potential even when you don't. Your Jambavan could be a mentor, a friend, or even a quiet inner voice urging you to rise to the occasion. Find them, and let them remind you of the greatness within.

Reflection: What Gifts Have You Left Behind?

Take a moment to pause and reflect. Ask yourself:

- *What did I love doing as a child?*
- *What activities make me lose track of time?*
- *What have others often complimented me on, even if I didn't see it as special?*

Write these thoughts down. Often, the answers to these questions are the breadcrumbs leading back to your gift.

Your Gift Is Not Just for You

Your gift is meant to be shared. It's not just about personal fulfilment; it's about the impact you can have on others. When you embrace your gift, you inspire others to do the same.

So, what's stopping you? Let's take the first step to rediscovering what's been waiting for you all along.

2

The Hidden Diamond Within You

Chapter Two

The Hidden Diamond Within You

"The greatest treasures are those invisible to the eye but found by the heart."

— Judy Garland

One day, a young boy approached his father with a question: *"What is the value of my life?"* Instead of giving him a straightforward answer, the father handed him a small, ordinary-looking rock. *"Take this rock,"* the father said, *"and go to the local market. If anyone asks for its price, simply raise two fingers and don't say a word."*

Puzzled but curious, the boy followed his father's instructions. At the market, a woman noticed the rock and exclaimed, *"How much is this? I'd love to put it in my garden!"* The boy, as instructed, raised two fingers. *"Two dollars?"* The woman asked. *"Perfect! I'll take it!"* The boy, surprised, hurried home and told his father, *"Someone wanted to buy this rock for $2!"*

His father smiled and said, *"Now, I want you to take this rock to the museum. Show it to them, and if anyone asks for its price, raise two fingers and don't say anything."*

The boy did as he was told. At the museum, a man studied the rock closely and said, *"This is unique. How much is it?"* The boy raised two fingers again. *"Two hundred dollars?"* The man replied. *"I'll buy it!"* Shocked, the boy ran home to his father and shouted, *"A man at the museum wanted to buy the rock for $200!"*

His father nodded and gave him one last task. *"Take this rock to the jewellerystore. Show it to the owner, and if he asks for its price, raise two fingers."* The boy, now eager to see what would happen, took the rock to the store. The owner's eyes widened with awe. *"Where did you find this? This is one of the rarest gems in the world!"* The boy raised two fingers, barely able to contain his excitement. *"Two hundred thousand dollars? I'll take it!"* The owner said.

The Hidden Diamond Within You   19

Overwhelmed, the boy rushed home and told his father, *"Someone offered $200,000 for this rock!"*

The father looked at his son and said, *"Now, do you see the value of your life?"*

THE LESSON: DISCOVERING YOUR TRUE WORTH

This story is a powerful reminder that *your value isn't defined by where you start, who surrounds you, or what others think of you.* Much like the rock, many of us carry incredible potential and hidden brilliance within us—our "diamond"—but we often live in places or situations where our worth is undervalued.

Imagine this: You might be like the $2 rock, stuck in a market where no one sees your brilliance. You might feel like just another person in the crowd, living an "ordinary" life because you've surrounded yourself with people who don't recognize the diamond within you. Perhaps you've settled for being small because that's what you've been told all your life.

But what happens when you change your environment? What happens when you surround yourself with people who see your true value—like the jeweller? Suddenly, your potential shines. Your strengths, talents, and gifts begin to glow like a rare gem.

The truth is: *Everybody has a diamond inside them.*

You have a gift—whether it's creativity, leadership, compassion, resilience, or an entirely unique skill. Just because you haven't been placed in the right environment yet, doesn't mean your value isn't extraordinary. Remember, *a diamond doesn't lose its value just because it's sitting in the wrong place.*

A CALL TO ACTION

As you reflect on this story, ask yourself:

- *Are you in a place that sees your worth? Or are you in the "$2 market" of life?*
- *Are you surrounding yourself with people who recognize the brilliance within you? Or are they holding you back?*
- *Most importantly, are you choosing to see the diamond within yourself?*

The moment you start believing in your true potential, you'll begin to shine. And when you help others see the diamonds within themselves, you'll light up the world.

Choose where you place yourself wisely. Choose the people around you carefully. And al-

ways remember: **You are far more valuable than you think.**

WHY WE STRUGGLE TO SEE OUR GIFTS

Just like the above story of boy holding a diamond in his hand. Imagine yourself in this position. If you've never seen a diamond before, you might dismiss it as just another rock. The same principle applies to our gifts. Because they come so naturally to us, we often fail to see their brilliance.

Society doesn't help either. We're conditioned to measure success by external standards—titles, paychecks, or approval from others. Rarely are we encouraged to look inward and discover what truly makes us unique.

But here's the truth: your gift is your compass. It's the thing you do so effortlessly that it often feels like play. It's what lights you up, even when the world feels heavy.

It's time to break free from the ordinary and let your brilliance shine. **The world is waiting to see your diamond.**

3

Breaking Free From The Invisible Rope

Breaking Free From The Invisible Rope

"Fortune favors the bold."

— Latin Proverb

In a quiet village, there was a small field where a lone horse stood, tethered to a wooden stake with a thin rope. This horse was majestic—strong, muscular, and powerful, capable of running with the wind and leaping over obstacles effortlessly. Yet, there it stood, unmoving and docile, as though the rope held it in place with unyielding force.

A passerby noticed the unusual sight and couldn't help but feel puzzled. He approached the horse's owner and asked, "Why doesn't this horse run away? The rope is so thin and the stake so small. Surely, it could break free with even the slightest pull."

The owner smiled knowingly and said, "This horse has been tied to a rope like this since it was a foal. Back then, the rope was strong enough to hold it, and no matter how much it pulled or struggled, it couldn't escape. After many attempts, the little horse gave up and accepted that it could never break free. Now that it's grown strong, it doesn't even try anymore. It still believes the rope is stronger than it is."

The passerby stared at the horse, stunned. This magnificent creature, capable of great strength and speed, remained bound—not by the rope itself, but by the belief it had carried since its youth. It was free to escape at any moment, yet it stayed still, unaware of its true power.

Invisible ropes—old fears and doubts—often hold us back long after we've outgrown them. Like the tethered horse, we need to challenge these limitations to discover our true strength.

For example, I see this in many of my friends who tremble at the mere thought of leaving their jobs or getting laid-off, despite having substantial financial security. They possess remarkable talents that could flourish in other professions or succeed in business ventures, yet they remain tethered to their corporate lives. Like the horse with its thin rope, they're bound not by actual limitations, but by the deeply ingrained belief that a steady job is their only path to security. They've become so conditioned to this way of life that even contemplating an alternative path fills them with paralyzing fear.

It's time to realize that the rope is not holding you back—your belief is. The moment you challenge it, you'll discover the strength within you to move beyond any limitation. Don't let an old rope keep you from running free. The world is waiting for you to embrace your true power and take that first bold step toward freedom.

BREAKING THE INVISIBLE ROPE

The first step to breaking free is recognizing that the rope exists only in your mind. It's not your capabilities that are holding you back—it's your perception of them. You have grown, evolved, and accumulated skills and strengths that make you far more powerful than you were when that belief first took hold.

Ask yourself:

- What's holding me back?
- Is this limitation real, or is it something I've accepted without question?
- What would happen if I tried, despite my fear or doubt?

A CALL TO COURAGE

Breaking free from these mental constraints requires courage. It's not easy to challenge beliefs that have been ingrained for years, or even decades. But the reward is immense. Once you break the invisible rope, you'll discover a world of possibilities, a strength you didn't know you had, and a life that's no longer confined by boundaries created in your mind.

Think about the real world. Imagine a corporate employee who has spent the last 10, 15, or even 20 years in the same job. Deep inside, they've always felt a calling—an urge to become a painter, singer, musician, entrepreneur, hotelier, coach, management guru, author, public speaker, politician, or even an actor. Yet, despite this calling, they remain in the same routine.

Why? Because breaking free is terrifying. Even when the job feels draining, leaving it feels like an impossible idea. After all, a steady paycheck at the start of every month, clearing EMIs, going on fancy vacations, and buying expensive things create a comfort zone that's hard to leave. The thought of stepping into the unknown feels daunting, overwhelming, and risky.

And it's true—there is struggle in breaking free.

When you finally decide to pursue your true calling, you'll find yourself battling years of rust that have settled over your natural talents. The process will require effort, persistence, and resilience. But here's the truth: only by walking through that struggle will you rediscover the brilliance of your God-given gifts. That is when glory truly embraces you.

As you read this, take a moment to think about the ropes that might be holding you back. Is it the fear of failure? The fear of rejection? The weight of societal expectations? The scars of past mistakes? Whatever it may be, know this: you have the power to break free.

The strength you need is already within you. The time has come to challenge those invisible ropes, to take that courageous first step, and to finally embrace the life you were always meant to live.

MOVING FORWARD

Just like the horse in this story—or like the ancient tale of Lord Hanuman, we sometimes need a reminder of our true strength. Remember, you were never meant to stay tethered. Your potential is vast, your power is real, and your life is waiting for you to claim it. Break the rope and take the first step toward your freedom—the superhero within you is ready to soar.

❖ ❖ ❖

4

The Fear of Flying: Overcoming Self-Doubt

 Chapter Fourth

The Fear of Flying
Overcoming Self-Doubt

"He who has overcome his fears will truly be free."

— Aristotle

The fear of flying is a powerful metaphor for the fear of failure, the fear of taking risks, and the fear of stepping into the unknown. Many of us are trapped by our internal doubts, paralyzed by the thought of what might go wrong. We hesitate to take action, thinking that our efforts will never be good enough. But in reality, the path to growth lies in facing those fears head-on and overcoming them.

THE STORY OF THE EAGLE AND THE SKY

Imagine a young eagle on its first flight. As it

stands at the edge of the cliff, looking at the vast sky, it feels a mix of excitement and fear. The eagle has never flown before, and the thought of soaring into the unknown is terrifying. What if it falls? What if it can't fly?

But despite these fears, the eagle leaps into the air. It flaps its wings, struggling at first, but soon finds its rhythm. The fear of falling starts to fade as the eagle gains confidence with every beat of its wings. Slowly, it realizes that the sky is not its enemy—it is its opportunity.

This story is a reminder that taking the first step, no matter how uncertain, is the key to overcoming self-doubt. Once you leap into the unknown, you'll discover strengths you never knew existed.

OVERCOMING THE FEAR OF FLYING

To overcome self-doubt, we need to acknowledge that fear is a natural part of the growth process. Every challenge, every fear we face is an opportunity to evolve. The key is to take action in spite of the fear.

Here are a few strategies to help you overcome self-doubt and take flight:

- Build Resilience: Resilience is built through repeated action.

- Surround Yourself with Support: Surround yourself with positive influences.

- Visualize Success: Imagine yourself flying, imagine yourself achieving your goals. Visualizing success creates a mental picture of what's possible, and this vision helps drive your actions.

BREAK THE CYCLE

During my MBA, one concept that truly fascinated me was **Breakthrough Management**. It emphasizes a crucial truth: when you find yourself stuck on a plateau — whether in your career, finances, or personal life — it's a warning sign that **stagnation is setting in**. And in most cases, stagnation is just a slow march toward decline. To **thrive**, you must recognize when you're trapped in a cycle and take decisive action to break free.

I've seen this firsthand with my friend **Ravi**. For years, he dreamed of **owning a home**, but every time his salary increased, **property prices in Mumbai surged even faster**, making his goal feel impossible. Frustrated with this endless loop, **he** decided to take control instead of waiting for circumstances to change.

He **relocated to Surat**, a thriving **tier-II city in India**, where real estate was far more affordable. But this move wasn't just about buying property— it was about **shifting his mindset and unlocking new opportunities.** In Surat, he landed a **better-paying job in a growing industry**, which not only **improved his finances** but also gave him **a better quality of life.** Within a year, he purchased a **sprawling home at one-third the price** of what he would have paid in Mumbai. The move that once felt risky turned out to be the best decision of his life.

This is the power of **breaking the cycle**. Sometimes, the key to success isn't working harder at the same problem—it's **changing the game entirely**. Whether it's **relocating, switching industries, or daring to take a different path**, the moment you break free from stagnation, new opportunities begin to appear.

Every bold step **builds confidence, resilience, and momentum**. So, if you ever feel stuck, **dare to disrupt your own patterns. Step outside your** comfort zone, take the leap, and watch yourself soar!

EMBRACING CHANGE

Breaking the cycle and overcoming self-doubt require courage and clarity. The lessons from the eagle and my friend's story illustrate a universal truth: progress begins the moment you decide to act. You don't have to take monumental steps right away — small, intentional actions can create the momentum needed to soar to new heights.

So, what's holding you back? Embrace the fear, challenge the status quo, and trust in your ability to navigate the unknown. The sky is vast, full of opportunities waiting for you to take flight. Let today be the day you decide to soar.

5

The Superhero Inside

Chapter Five

The Superhero Inside

"Our doubts are traitors and make us lose the good we oft might win, by fearing to attempt."

— William Shakespeare

Throughout life, many of us wander in search of meaning, unaware of the extraordinary gifts we carry inside. Just like the character of David Dunn in UNBREAKABLE, we often fail to recognize the potential that resides within us until it is revealed by a significant event or the right guidance.

The Story of David Dunn

David Dunn, a seemingly ordinary man, had lived a life full of struggles. He worked as a security guard, a job he accepted with little enthusiasm or fulfillment. His life, much like many others, was a routine—a series of mundane events that made him feel disconnected from any greater purpose. David had no idea that he was living with a secret power, a gift that could change everything.

It wasn't until a tragic accident on a train that the truth about David's abilities began to surface. The crash, which claimed the lives of many, left David unscathed. He walked away from the wreckage without a scratch. His first hint of something extraordinary was a brief, almost dismissive moment. He attributed it to luck. But it wasn't luck—it was something deeper, something inside him.

For years, David had lived without fully understanding the significance of his strength. He had never asked himself why he could survive accidents that would have crushed others. His body was indestructible, capable of withstanding physical trauma that should have been fatal. But he had spent his life playing small—hiding behind the shadows of a regular, unremarkable existence. He never questioned why he never got sick, why he could lift heavy objects without effort, or why he had an uncanny ability to sense danger.

The Superhero Inside

David's life had been guided by self-doubt. He couldn't see the potential he held, because he had never been shown it. He continued in the same job, never challenging the idea that this was all he was meant to do. He was content with a life of mediocrity, never suspecting that he was destined for something far greater.

THE MOMENT OF REALIZATION: UNVEILING THE HERO WITHIN

It wasn't until he met Elijah Price, a man who had been researching people with special abilities, then David started to understand the power he had within. Elijah, who had spent his life uncovering the truth about people with unique gifts, saw the greatness in David long before he did. Elijah acted as a mirror, reflecting back to David the hero he had been blind to.

As Elijah explained, David began to see his abilities in a new light. His invincibility wasn't a fluke or coincidence—it was a sign of something greater. He wasn't just a regular man. He was a superhero, capable of using his powers for something meaningful. With this realization, David's entire perspective shifted. He could choose to embrace his superpowers or continue living a life of doubt and self-denial.

THE POWER OF EMBRACING YOUR TRUE POTENTIAL

David's journey mirrors the story of many of us. Like David, we may spend much of our lives unaware of our gifts. We might have talents, abilities, or qualities that set us apart, but we fail to recognize them because we don't know how to value them. We play small, living lives of quiet desperation, thinking that we are ordinary, when in fact, we are far from it.

The Power Of Awareness

Just as David had to learn to recognize his own power, we too must come to terms with our gifts. We all have something special inside us—whether it's resilience, creativity, kindness, or the ability to inspire others. But just like David, we often don't see it. We are caught up in the noise of everyday life, the struggle to fit in, and the pressure to conform to societal standards.

David's realization was a moment of awakening. And this is exactly what you need to do: recognize the treasure inside you. It's time to stop settling for mediocrity and start living the life you were meant to live.

THE STEPS TO RECOGNIZING YOUR SUPERPOWER

1. **Acknowledge Your Potential**: Reflect on the strengths you might have overlooked or underestimated.

2. **Stop Playing Small**: Stop hiding behind your fears and insecurities.

3. **Embrace Your Superpowers**: Once you recognize your gifts, use them! Don't let your talents sit idle. Whether it's in your personal life, career, or relationships, use your abilities to make a difference

THE LESSON: YOU ARE THE HERO OF YOUR OWN STORY

David Dunn spent much of his life unaware of his true potential. He lived with self-doubt, convinced that he was ordinary, when in fact, he was extraordinary. The moment he recognized his power was the moment his life began to transform.

Embrace your uniqueness, celebrate it, and take the steps necessary to unlock your true potential.

Your superpowers are waiting to be unleashed.

❖ ❖ ❖

6

Some Birds Aren't Meant to Be Caged

Chapter Six

Some Birds Aren't Meant to Be Caged

"Some birds aren't meant to be caged. Their feathers are just too bright. And when they fly away, the part of you that knows it was a sin to lock them up, does rejoice."

Few years back, I was watching movie, IMDB Rank #1, *The Shawshank Redemption*. The story's beginning is tragic, depicting how the main hero, Andy Dufresne, got wrongfully jailed. But with sheer determination and an indomitable spirit, he managed to break free from the prison—an almost impossible task—and went on to live a life of freedom, anonymously basking in the joy of being unshackled.

How many times in our lives do we find ourselves trapped in a cage we never chose? It could be a wrong job, a mismatched relationship, or an unfulfilling lifestyle. Like Andy, we continue to live in these figurative prisons, feeling the weight of confinement yet often lacking the courage to break out.

When Andy finally gains his freedom, his closest friend, Ellis Boyd "Red" Redding, reflects on his journey and utters these profoundly powerful words in the movie, reminding us of the beauty and necessity of breaking free from what confines us.

This sentiment strikes at the heart of what it means to embrace your true self. It's a call to action for every individual who feels trapped by circumstance, expectation, or fear. Just like Andy found his freedom, it's time to break your own cage.

Yet so many of us live our lives behind invisible bars, shackled by fear, guilt, and a desire to conform. It's easier to fit in than to stand out. It's safer to stay in the cage, to live quietly within the boundaries of what is expected of us, than to spread our wings and risk the unknown.

But what if the cage is only an illusion? What if the superhero within you has always been there, waiting for the moment you choose to step out and embrace your truth?

THE CAGE OF COMFORT AND EXPECTATIONS

Like the proverbial bird, many of us are placed into a "comfortable" cage early in life. We're told to follow the rules, play it safe, and stay within the confines of what society deems "normal." We're conditioned to believe that living small is a virtue, that it's better to live quietly than to disrupt the status quo.

The truth is, the cage is often built from fear—fear of failure, fear of judgment, fear of stepping into the unknown. It's not made of steel; it's made of stories we've been told and have come to believe. These stories convince us that we're not strong enough, not talented enough, or not deserving of a life outside the ordinary.

BREAKING FREE: THE MOMENT OF TRUTH

Every superhero has an origin story—a moment when they realize they're not ordinary, that they're meant for something greater. For some, this realization comes early in life. For others, it comes after years of struggle, self-doubt, and feeling trapped.

The moment you decide to break free is the moment you begin to live your truth. It doesn't mean abandoning all responsibilities or throwing caution to the wind. It means acknowledging that the cage doesn't define you, and that you have the power to choose freedom over fear.

Think of Andy Dufresne. Though falsely imprisoned, he never let the walls of the prison define his spirit. His famous words, "Get busy living, or get busy dying," remind us that the choice to live fully is always ours.

EMBRACING THE BRIGHT FEATHERS

The world needs your "bright feathers." Your unique gifts, talents, and perspectives are what make you extraordinary. But to share those gifts, you must first embrace them yourself. You must see your brilliance and believe in it, even when others can't.

Living your truth doesn't mean you'll never face challenges. The world isn't always kind to those who dare to fly higher. But the freedom, joy, and fulfillment that come from living authentically far outweigh the struggles of staying caged.

YOUR SUPERPOWER IS IN YOUR TRUTH

The superhero within you thrives on truth. It's not about being perfect; it's about being real. It's about standing tall in the face of adversity, trusting your instincts, and owning your unique path.

Some birds aren't meant to be caged, and neither are you. It's time to spread your wings, embrace your gifts, and live a life that reflects the incredible person you are.

WHEN BRIGHT FEATHERS TAKE FLIGHT

How often do we find ourselves trapped in routines dictated by others? Our hearts whisper of extraordinary possibilities, yet we choose to stay confined by comfort and obligation

But when someone finally breaks free, something remarkable happens: those around them suddenly acknowledge the brilliance they always saw but never mentioned. It's a common story in the corporate world—exceptional talents confined to mediocre roles, until the day they spread their wings and soar.

Consider these transformative journeys:

Chetan Bhagat (IIM Ahmedabad) and Amish Tripathi (IIM Calcutta) left their banking careers to become bestselling authors

Sachin Bansal and Rohit Bansal (IIT Delhi) transformed from corporate employees to revolutionizing Indian e-commerce with Flipkart and Snapdeal

R Madhavan evolved from an engineer to becoming one of India's most versatile actors

Dinesh Agarwal (HBTI Kanpur) left HCL Technologies to build IndiaMART, India's largest B2B marketplace, transforming business in India

These individuals share a common thread—they recognized that their "feathers were too bright" for conventional cages. Had they never heeded their inner calling, they might have lived comfortable but unfulfilled lives. Instead, they chose to embrace their gifts and found extraordinary success.

When you feel that stirring within—that whisper urging you toward something greater—remember these bright feathers who dared to fly. Your gift, like theirs, might be waiting for its moment to shine.

❖ ❖ ❖

7

The Road Less Chosen

Chapter Seven

The Road Less Chosen

"Two roads diverged in a wood, and I—I took the one less travelled by, and that has made all the difference."

— Robert Frost

I still remember long back I was reading the newspaper, an advertisement for BMW immediately caught my attention. It featured the above powerful quote in its advertisement.

The message behind the ad was more than just about driving a luxury car; it spoke of success, courage, and the power of choice. It resonated deeply because it symbolized something we all encounter in life—moments where we stand at a crossroads. Those who achieve true success, fulfilment, and meaning are often the ones who choose the unconventional path. They dare to take the road less travelled, not because it is easier, but because it offers something greater: the promise of purpose.

The image of a diverging road reflects the choices we all must make. Do we follow the crowd and walk down the familiar path, or do we forge our own way, guided by our values, dreams, and aspirations? The road less travelled is not always smooth, and often it is met with resistance, doubt, and uncertainty. But this path holds the greatest rewards—it's where we discover who we truly are and what we are capable of.

The ad was not just about a car; it was about a mindset. It reminded me, and now I remind you, that every decision we make shapes the journey of our life. When you choose the path less taken, you are choosing to step outside your comfort zone, to trust your instincts, and to embrace your unique journey. And in doing so, you unlock possibilities that conformity could never offer.

So, as you reflect on your own crossroads, ask yourself: *Are you willing to take the road less chosen?* It might not be the easiest choice, but it just might make all the difference in your life.

In life, we often face decisions that require us to take a leap of faith. Sometimes, the choices seem clear, because they are aligned with the expectations of society, family, or peers. Other times, the path before us is less certain, filled with challenges and uncertainty, but it offers the possibility of something extraordinary. It is here, at the crossroads of certainty and possibility, where true success is born.

WHY PEOPLE AVOID THE ROAD LESS CHOSEN

There are many reasons why people avoid the road less chosen. Fear of failure, fear of judgment, and the comfort of familiarity can all keep us from stepping into the unknown. Many people stay in jobs they dislike, live lives that feel unfulfilled, or avoid pursuing their dreams because the road ahead seems too risky.

But here's the truth: success rarely comes from taking the easy road. The road less travelled requires you to step out of your comfort zone, face challenges head-on, and trust in your own abilities. It asks you to believe in yourself when others may not see your potential. And it is often through these struggles that we discover our true strength and achieve what we once thought impossible.

THE REWARDS OF TAKING THE ROAD LESS CHOSEN

The rewards of this path are rarely immediate, but they are deeply fulfilling and often life-changing. Think about those who have made history—great innovators, leaders, and thinkers. They were not the ones who followed the crowd. They were the ones who questioned the status quo, who took risks, and who chose a path that others considered too difficult or uncertain. These people did not find success because they were lucky; they found it because they had the courage to choose a different path and persist in the face of adversity.

Take, for example, the rise of modern-day content creators and YouTubers. A few years ago, when they chose to step away from traditional career paths and follow their instincts, many faced doubt and judgment from family, friends, and society. In a world where success is often measured by stable jobs or conventional sources of income, their decision to pursue an unconventional dream was met with skepticism.

But here we are now, — YouTubers, once considered to be engaging in "unserious" or "non-credible" work, are earning millions, influencing global audiences, and becoming celebrities in their own right. They chose to believe in their passions when no one else did. They embraced the discomfort of uncertainty and dared to take the road less chosen.

THE LESSON: DARE TO CHOOSE DIFFERENTLY

If you want to achieve something extraordinary in life, you must be willing to make choices that others may not understand. Choosing the road less travelled isn't always easy, but it is often the most rewarding. The world is full of people who follow the same old paths, chasing after the same old goals. To truly stand out and make a difference, you must be willing to walk in the direction that feels right for you—even if it means taking the path less chosen by others.

When you walk your own path, you begin to live authentically, to align your actions with your true self, and to pursue goals that resonate with your heart. It is through this authenticity that you will find true fulfilment and success.

ACTION STEPS:

1. **Identify the Crossroads in Your Life**: Reflect on the moments when you've faced

choices. Which path did you choose? Were you swayed by external expectations, or did you follow your own intuition? If you're at a crossroads now, what path is calling you?

2. **Let Go of Fear and Doubt**: Fear is often what holds us back from taking the road less chosen. Let go of the fear of judgment, failure, and the unknown. Believe in yourself and your ability to succeed.

3. **Walk Your Unique Path**: Remember that your journey is yours alone. It may not look like anyone else's, and that's okay. Focus on what feels right for you, and take the steps necessary to bring your dreams to life.

❖ ❖ ❖

8

The Unseen Force Around You: Notice your energy

Chapter Eight

The Unseen Force Around You: Notice your energy

"With great power comes great responsibility."

— Voltaire

Have you ever noticed something unusual? You walk into a shop, and shortly after, more customers begin to arrive. It happens again and again, and at first, you brush it off as a coincidence. But what if it's not? What if there's something deeper at play—something about *you* that draws others in?

Whether you realize it or not, the energy you carry—the positive aura you emit—has the power to influence the world around you. People feel your presence before you even speak, and your energy becomes a silent magnet, attracting others to you.

YOUR INVISIBLE INFLUENCE

This unseen force is more than just charm or luck. It's an inherent part of who you are—a blend of your aura, your charisma, and your authenticity. Much like David Dunn from the movie Unbreakable, who slowly discovers his hidden strength, we all carry an invisible power within us. It might not be as visible as physical strength, but its impact is undeniable.

Think of the times people have told you, "You have such a positive vibe," or commented on your ability to uplift others without trying. This energy might feel so natural to you that you barely notice it, but those around you certainly do. It's not luck or coincidence—it's the influence of your true self radiating outward.

The shopkeeper may not know why customers flock in after your arrival. You might not fully understand it yourself. But this unseen force—the energy you project—has the power to shape the world around you, even when you don't realize it.

THE STORY OF SUHANI SHAH

Consider Suhani Shah, a modern-day mind reader and mentalist. From a young age, Suhani noticed something extraordinary about herself. While most children were immersed in conventional academics, she found herself drawn to the art of connecting with people on a deeper level. Her natural ability to understand unspoken emotions and thoughts became evident early in her life.

Unlike others who might dismiss such a gift, Suhani embraced it with curiosity and determination. She began honing her skills, performing her first stage show at the age of seven. It wasn't just her ability to read minds that set her apart—it was the magnetic energy she carried, an aura that drew people in and made them feel seen and understood.

Suhani's journey teaches us that recognizing and embracing our energy can unlock new levels of influence and impact. By leaning into her gift, she turned her passion into a remarkable career, captivating audiences and inspiring wonder wherever she went. Her story bears witness to early self-awareness and the courage to follow an unconventional path.

BECOMING THE LIGHT YOU WERE MEANT TO BE

The key to unlocking this potential is awareness. The energy you carry—your aura—is a powerful force. It's easy to dismiss it as coincidence or chance, but when you recognize it for what it truly is, it becomes a tool for creating change.

Imagine walking into a room, knowing that your presence alone can uplift and inspire. Your energy can spark opportunities, motivate others, and help those around you discover their own potential. Once you embrace this unseen force, you can channel it to impact not only your life but also the lives of those you touch.

ACTION STEPS:

1. **Observe Your Energy:** Take a few moments each day to notice the energy you bring to situations. How do people respond when you're present? Are they drawn to you? Do they seem more positive, relaxed, or engaged?

2. **Harness Your Aura:** Once you recognize your power, begin using it intentionally. Set clear intentions before entering situations, and use your energy to create positive outcomes.

3. **Share Your Positive Energy:** Instead of hoarding your energy, share it with others.

Be the source of light in a room, the spark that inspires and motivates. The more you give, the more your aura will grow.

❖ ❖ ❖

9

It's Never Too Late

Chapter Nine

It's Never Too Late

"Success is not final, failure is not fatal: It is the courage to continue that counts."

— Winston Churchill

Life doesn't always unfold according to a neatly designed plan. For some, the journey toward self-discovery and success is a slow burn—a process that takes time, effort, and sometimes, a series of missteps. It's easy to feel disheartened when you see others achieving great things at a young age. But the truth is, it's not the age at which you begin that matters; it's the moment when you recognize your true potential and step into your greatness.

There are countless stories of people who discovered their unique abilities later in life, and the impact they made was not only significant—it was transformational. Think of Raymond Kroc, who was

52 when he bought McDonald's and turned it into the worldwide fast-food phenomenon we know today.

In the artistic realm and closer to modern times, BomanIrani offers another inspiring example. After working as a photographer and managing a small wafer shop, he discovered his passion for acting in his 40s. His breakout role in Munna Bhai M.B.B.S. catapulted him to fame, and he became one of the most versatile and beloved actors in Indian cinema.

And then there's the remarkable story of J.K. Rowling, who was 32 years old, broke, and struggling as a single mother when she conceived the idea for Harry Potter. She faced rejection from multiple publishers but kept pushing forward, driven by her passion and belief in her story. Eventually, her perseverance paid off, and the Harry Potter series became a global phenomenon, inspiring millions and transforming her life overnight. Rowling's journey stands as powerful proof of the impact of late discoveries and the magic that happens when you believe in your gift.

These stories remind us that life doesn't come with a deadline for success. Whether you're in your 30s, 40s, 50s, or beyond, your moment can come when you're ready to embrace it. It's never too late to uncover your true potential and make your mark on the world.

WHY IT'S NEVER TOO LATE

It's easy to feel disheartened when others around you seem to be achieving their dreams while you're still figuring out your path. Society often places pressure on individuals to have their life figured out by a certain age. But the truth is that success isn't about following a strict timeline—it's about understanding that your unique gifts can emerge at any point in your life. The key is to stay open to the possibility of discovery, even if it comes later than you expected.

Age does not determine your potential. What matters is your ability to recognize your gift and pursue it with passion, regardless of the stage in life you're at. BomanIrani found his calling in his 40s and in doing so, he proved that it's never too late to make an impact.

TURNING YOUR LATE DISCOVERY INTO SUCCESS

If you've only recently begun to recognize your own gifts, or if you're in a place where you feel like time is running out, remember this: The world doesn't need you to have everything figured out by a certain age. You don't have to be famous or rich by the time you're 30, 40, or even 50. What matters is that you identify your potential and take steps toward utilizing it.

Here are a few things you can do to ensure that your later discovery becomes your greatest strength:

1. **Embrace Your Journey :** Every step you've taken up until now, even the failures, have led you to this moment of discovery. Embrace the path you've walked—it has shaped you into who you are today.

2. **Don't Fear the Late Start :** A late start doesn't mean you're behind. It just means that your journey is unfolding at its own pace. You have time to learn, grow, and flourish at a speed that works for you.

3. **Keep Pursuing Your Passion :** Like Rowlings, it's essential to believe in your gift, even when others don't see it yet. Stay committed to your passions and keep pushing forward, even when the road seems tough.

THE STORY OF J.K. ROWLING: FROM ROCK BOTTOM TO A MAGICAL LEGACY

At **32 years old**, **J.K. Rowling** was at one of the lowest points in her life. She was a **single mother**, recently divorced, struggling to make ends meet while living on government welfare in a tiny apartment in **Edinburgh, Scotland**. She had no stable job, barely enough money to feed her daughter, and was battling **clinical depression**. At one point, she even considered herself a failure.

But amid this darkness, she held onto **one thing—her love for storytelling**.

She had first conceived the idea of HARRY POTTER years earlier while on a delayed train ride. The story of a young orphan boy discovering he was a wizard filled her mind, and she knew she had to write it. But life kept getting in the way—personal struggles, financial troubles, and self-doubt all slowed her progress. Still, **she refused to let go of her dream**.

She wrote whenever she could—scribbling notes on napkins in cafes while her daughter slept in a stroller. When she finally completed HARRY POTTER AND THE PHILOSOPHER'S STONE, she sent the manuscript to publishers. **And was rejected.**

Again. And again. Twelve publishers turned her down, telling her that a **fantasy book for children wouldn't sell.**

Most people would have given up. But **Rowling didn't**.

She **kept pushing forward**, believing in the story she had created. Finally, a small publishing house, **Bloomsbury**, agreed to take a chance on her book. Even then, they advised her to **get a day job** because they didn't think she'd make much money as a children's author.

But then, the **magic happened**.

HARRY POTTER AND THE PHILOSOPHER'S STONE became an **instant sensation**. The book series went on to sell over **500 million copies**, making it one of the **best-selling book franchises in history**. The **Harry Potter** universe expanded into movies, theme parks, merchandise, and an entire cultural phenomenon that continues to inspire millions around the world.

Rowling, who once **struggled to afford heating in her home**, became the **first author in history to reach billionaire status** through book sales alone.

It's Never Too Late

THE LESSON: IT'S NEVER TOO LATE TO CHASE YOUR DREAM

J.K. Rowling's story proves that **there is no deadline for success.** She wasn't a child prodigy, she didn't achieve fame in her twenties, and she had no privileges to fall back on. She was simply **a woman with a story, a passion, and an unshakable belief in herself.**

Had she given up after her first rejection, the world would never have known Harry Potter. Had she let financial struggles or self-doubt stop her, she wouldn't have built the incredible legacy she has today.

Like Winston Churchill's quote:

"Success is not final, failure is not fatal: It is the courage to continue that counts."

If you ever feel like it's **too late** to start something new, remember **J.K. Rowling's journey.** Whether you're **30, 40, 50, or beyond**, your story is still **unfolding.** The world needs your gifts—**but only if you have the courage to share them.**

DON'T BE AN ETERNAL PROCRASTINATOR

Procrastination is a silent thief of dreams. Many people spend years thinking, "I'll do this once I have more time," or "I'll chase my passion when life gets less busy." But here's the hard truth: there will never be a "perfect time." This mindset often becomes a mental blockage—an endless cycle of waiting and postponing that stretches for years, even decades.

A STORY OF BREAKING FREE FROM PROCRASTINATION

I once had a friend named Arjun who always talked about starting his own café. He loved cooking, experimenting with flavours, and had a flair for hospitality that made people feel instantly at home. But every time he thought about taking the leap, his mind was flooded with reasons to delay—he wasn't financially ready, the market seemed too competitive, and he felt he needed more experience.

For years, Arjun juggled a corporate job that paid the bills but drained his passion. One day, after yet another conversation about his café dream, a close mentor told him, "Arjun, the best time to start was five years ago. The second-best time is now. If you wait for the stars to align, you'll wait forever."

That conversation struck a chord. Arjun decided to stop waiting and took the first step—he started hosting small pop-up dinners from his home on weekends. The response was overwhelming, and within a year, he had saved enough money and gained enough confidence to open his café. Today, it's a thriving space where people gather not just for food, but for the warmth and experience he always envisioned.

THE LESSON: START NOW

Scientific studies reveal that one of the biggest regrets people have near the end of their lives is not attempting the things they always wanted to do. It's not the failures they regret, but the dreams they never pursued. The time to act is now. Don't let procrastination rob you of the chance to live the life you've always envisioned. Be an action-taker. Start small, but start. The world is waiting for you to step into your potential.

FINAL THOUGHTS: IT'S NEVER TOO LATE TO START

Remember, your journey toward discovering your unique abilities doesn't have a deadline. Like J.K. Rowling, you may find that your greatest success happens later in life. It's not the age at which you start; it's the courage, belief, and persistence you bring to the pursuit of your passion.

Keep searching, stay open, and continue to trust in the process. The best chapters of your life may still be ahead of you.

❖ ❖ ❖

10

The Danger of Aiming Too Low

Chapter Ten

The Danger of Aiming Too Low

"The greater danger for most of us lies not in setting our aim too high and falling short, but in setting our aim too low, and achieving our mark."

- Michelangelo

Many of us continue living ordinary lives—not because we lack the capacity for greatness, but because we have accepted "good enough" as our default. We settle. We tell ourselves that comfort is better than the risk of failure, that the life we have is acceptable even if it doesn't inspire us. In doing so, we often overlook the incredible, god-given gifts we carry.

This profound truth reflects the invisible chains of complacency. How often do we choose smaller dreams because they seem easier to achieve? How many talents go undiscovered because we're content with mediocrity? Perhaps you've felt that quiet nagging voice inside, urging you to aim higher, but you've silenced it with excuses of stability, safety, or fear

WHY DO WE SETTLE FOR LESS?

The root cause of settling lies in comfort and doubt. When we aim too low:

1. **We avoid the risk of failure** – Failure feels like a rejection of our efforts, so we shrink our dreams to avoid it.

2. **We fear judgment** – What if others think we're too ambitious or unrealistic?

3. **We believe our gifts are ordinary** – If something comes naturally to us, we assume it's not special enough to pursue.

But greatness is never born from comfort. It's born from daring to dream beyond what we think is possible. Think about the people who inspire you the most—visionaries, artists, leaders—they were never content with average. They aimed high, knowing the risk of falling short, but understanding the greater danger of never trying at all.

RISE ABOVE THE ORDINARY

Living a meaningful life means striving for your highest potential. Don't fall into the trap of achieving small goals while ignoring your greater purpose. Remember, it's not arrogance to believe you are destined for more. It's self-awareness.

So, today, take Michelangelo's words to heart. Raise your aim. Stretch your goals. Challenge yourself to pursue the extraordinary, even if it feels uncomfortable at first. You were not created to live a life of small victories. You were made to soar.

THE STORY OF SIR EDMUND HILLARY: CONQUERING EVEREST AGAINST ALL ODDS

For centuries, **Mount Everest,** the tallest mountain in the world, stood as an **unconquerable giant.** Many had attempted to climb it, but no one had ever reached its **8,849-meter (29,032 feet) peak** and lived to tell the tale. Some believed it was **impossible,** that humans were simply **not meant to survive at such extreme heights.**

But one man dared to challenge the impossible— Sir Edmund Hillary.

A JOURNEY OF RELENTLESS DETERMINATION

Hillary was **not born a prodigy.** He was an ordinary

beekeeper from New Zealand, with no extraordinary physical gifts. But he had an **unstoppable will** and a belief that **no goal was too high.**

In 1953, Hillary, along with **Tenzing Norgay,** a skilled Sherpa climber, joined an expedition to conquer Everest. The journey was brutal—**freezing temperatures, hurricane-force winds, and the constant risk of avalanches.** Many before them had turned back, their bodies unable to withstand the lack of oxygen at such altitudes.

At one point, when asked if he thought Everest could be climbed, Hillary responded, "**It is not the mountain we conquer, but ourselves.**"

And on **May 29, 1953, Hillary and Tenzing became the first humans to reach the summit of Everest.**

THE WORLD'S PERSPECTIVE CHANGED FOREVER

Before Hillary, people thought **climbing Everest was beyond human limits.** But once he did it, others began to believe. Within the next few decades, **thousands of climbers followed in his footsteps.**

His achievement proved one simple truth: **The only**

The Danger of Aiming Too Low

true limits in life are the ones we accept.

THE LESSON: ARE YOU LIMITING YOURSELF?

Hillary's story teaches us that **our greatest limitations are not external,** but internal. Many people settle for "small goals" because they believe that's all they can achieve. They don't even attempt greatness because it **seems too difficult, too far, too risky.**

But like Hillary, **what if you aimed for something extraordinary?**

- What if you didn't settle for "good enough"?
- What if you stopped fearing failure and started believing in your true potential?

Most people choose to stay at the base of the mountain—**comfortable, safe, average. Few dare to climb.** But those who do? **They are the ones who change history.**

So, what's your Everest?

Don't let fear or doubt hold you back. **Set your sights high, take the first step, and keep climbing.** Because, as Hillary proved, the only real limits are the ones you refuse to challenge.

❖ ❖ ❖

11

The Ripple Effect of Your Superpower

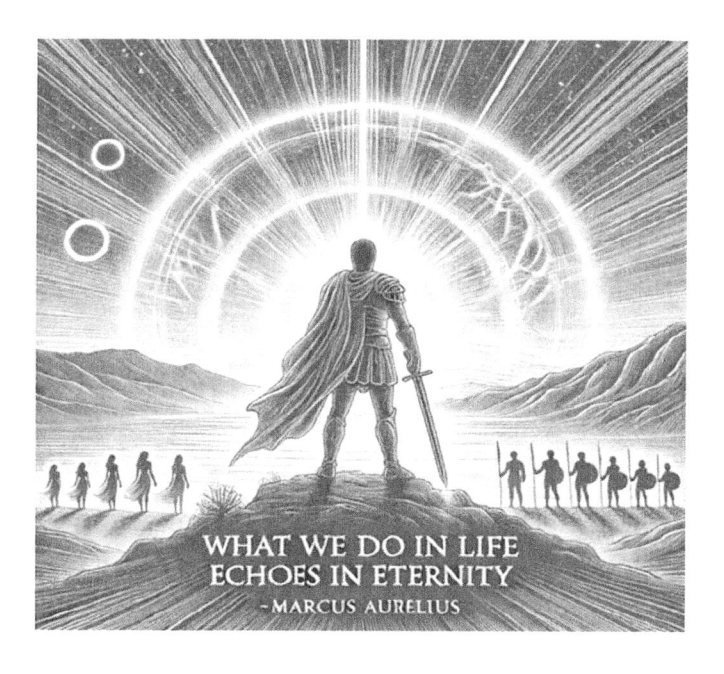

WHAT WE DO IN LIFE
ECHOES IN ETERNITY
-MARCUS AURELIUS

Chapter Eleven

The Ripple Effect of Your Superpower

"What we do in life echoes in eternity"

– Marcus Aurelius

The first time I heard this quote was while watching Gladiator. In the opening scene, as General Maximus prepares his army for battle, he turns to his soldiers and delivers these words with unwavering conviction. That moment struck me deeply. It wasn't just a cinematic line—it was a truth that transcended time, resonating with the very essence of what it means to leave a lasting impact.

This quote reminded me of something we often forget: the actions we take today, no matter how small, have the power to create ripples that extend far beyond our immediate surroundings. We tend to underestimate the influence of our choices, assuming that our efforts are insignificant in the grand scheme of things. But in reality, every decision, every act of kindness, every moment of courage contributes to something greater than ourselves.

Your unique gift, when harnessed, doesn't just transform your own life—it has the power to inspire, uplift, and shape the lives of others in ways you may never fully realize. Like an echo that continues long after the words have been spoken, the energy you put into the world—through your actions, your beliefs, and your purpose—creates waves that will reach places you may never see.

So, what will your echo be? Will it be one of hesitation and fear, or one of action and impact? The choice is yours, and the world is waiting for the ripple effect of your superpower.

THE POWER OF SMALL ACTIONS

Imagine throwing a small stone into a calm pond. The initial splash is minimal, but the ripples continue to expand, touching every corner of the water. These ripples represent the far-reaching effects of your actions and decisions. Your superpower—whether it's kindness, creativity, leadership, or resilience—can have a similar impact.

Sometimes we are hesitant to act because we believe that our contributions are too small to matter. But when we recognize that every action, no matter how small, can spark a chain reaction, we begin to see how interconnected we are with the world around us.

YOUR SUPERPOWER IS NOT JUST FOR YOU

In a similar way, your superpower isn't just for you — it is a gift to the world. Every time you use your unique abilities to create positive change, whether through your work, relationships, or community, you inspire others to do the same. The energy you put into the world amplifies, creating a ripple effect that can change lives.

THE RIPPLE EFFECT IN YOUR LIFE

One act of courage can inspire someone else to face their fears. One word of encouragement can lift someone up from despair. One creative idea can spark an entire movement. Your superpower isn't meant to be hoarded or hidden — it's meant to be shared, to grow, and to transform the world around you.

THE RIPPLE EFFECT OF ONE TEACHER: THE STORY OF DR. ABDUL KALAM AND HIS MENTOR

Dr. A.P.J. Abdul Kalam, India's beloved scientist and former President, often spoke about the profound impact his teacher, **SivasubramaniaIyer,** had on his life. Growing up in a humble town in Rameswaram, young Kalam was a curious and ambitious boy with dreams bigger than his circumstances.

One day, during a science lesson, his teacher wanted to explain **how birds fly.** Instead of just using a textbook, Iyer took Kalam and his classmates to the beach. He pointed at the birds in the sky and explained the concepts of lift, drag, and aerodynamics in a way that captured young Kalam's imagination. It was in that moment that Kalam realized his passion for **aerospace and aviation**—a dream that led him to become one of the most celebrated scientists in India, spearheading the nation's missile and space programs.

Decades later, when Kalam became the President of India, he often credited that one teacher for **igniting his mind** and setting him on a path that changed not just his life, but the future of an entire nation. That single act of a teacher's passion **rippled out**—from inspiring one boy to shaping India's space and defense advancements, touching the lives of millions.

The Ripple Effect of Your Superpower

THE POWER OF A SINGLE ACTION

SivasubramaniaIyer probably didn't realize at the time that his simple lesson at the beach would set into motion a legacy that would **echo through eternity.** But that is the power of small actions—they grow beyond our imagination.

You, too, have the ability to influence lives in ways you may never fully realize. Whether it's a kind word, a shared idea, or a moment of encouragement, your impact doesn't stop with you. **It travels forward, inspiring others to take action, to dream bigger, and to create change.**

Like Dr.Kalam's teacher, you might one day find that a small action—something you said, did, or shared—was the spark that changed someone's life forever. **Your superpower is not just for you. It is meant to inspire and empower those around you.**

THE LESSON: YOU HAVE THE POWER TO CREATE POSITIVE CHANGE

Your superpower, no matter how big or small, has the potential to create a lasting impact. Every time you choose to act with intention, to use your gift to benefit others, you create ripples that extend far beyond what you can imagine.

Don't underestimate the power of your actions. When you embrace your superpower and share it with the world, you become a catalyst for change, lighting the way for others to follow. The world needs your gifts more than ever.

❖ ❖ ❖

12

Legacy : Leaving the World a Better Place

Chapter Twelve

Legacy : Leaving the World a Better Place

"Someone is sitting in the shade today because someone planted a tree a long time ago."

— Warren Buffett

We all have a unique gift, but it's not enough to simply discover it. What truly matters is how we use that gift to create something lasting and meaningful. Every superhero—whether they realize it or not—has the potential to leave behind a legacy. The impact we have on the world, the people we touch, and the difference we make can endure long after we're gone.

Take a moment to think about the word "legacy." For many, it conjures up images of grand monuments, famous names, or monumental achievements. But a legacy doesn't have to be something that's universally recognized or measured in terms of fame or fortune. It can simply be the positive influence you have on the people around you. The good you do in the world, no matter how small, creates ripples that extend far beyond what you can see.

CREATING A LEGACY OF IMPACT

To leave a legacy that is truly meaningful, you must first ask yourself: What kind of impact do I want to have? Do you want to be remembered for your kindness, your creativity, your leadership, or the way you helped others? A legacy is created through intentional action, and it is shaped by the way you choose to live each day.

THE GOOD MAHARAJA: THE INDIAN KING WHO SHELTERED POLISH ORPHANS DURING WWII

During World War II, as the world was consumed by destruction and despair, Maharaja DigvijaysinhjiRanjitsinhjiJadeja of Jamnagar displayed an extraordinary act of compassion by saving the lives of over 1,000 Polish children who had escaped Nazi and Soviet persecution.

A JOURNEY OF DESPERATION

After Poland was invaded by Germany and the Soviet Union in 1939, thousands of Polish families were forcibly deported to labor camps. Many perished. The lucky few who survived embarked on a perilous journey through Russia, Iran, and other war-torn lands, desperately searching for safety. Most countries turned them away, unwilling or unable to offer shelter during the global conflict.

A KING'S COMPASSION

When Maharaja Digvijaysinhji learned about these suffering children, he did not hesitate—he offered them a home in India. In Balachadi, near Jamnagar (present-day Gujarat, India), he built a refugee camp where these children were given food, shelter, education, and—above all—a sense of belonging. He reassured them:

"Do not consider yourself orphans. You are now Nawangarians, and I am Bapu (father) to all of you."

For years, he cared for them like his own, giving them a second chance at life. Even after the war ended, many of these children carried his kindness in their hearts forever.

A FUTURE PRIME MINISTER AMONG THEM

One of these children, Bogdan Borusewicz, who had been among the Polish refugees in India, later grew up to become the Speaker of the Polish Senate and Acting Prime Minister of Poland. His journey—from an orphaned refugee to a leader of his nation—symbolizes the incredible ripple effect of Maharaja Digvijaysinhji's selfless act.

THE LESSON: TRUE LEGACY IS MEASURED BY LIVES TOUCHED

Maharaja Digvijaysinhji didn't conquer lands or expand his kingdom, yet his greatest achievement was in saving innocent lives. His legacy is written not in history books alone, but in the hearts of those he helped.

Like Warren Buffett's quote:

"Someone is sitting in the shade today because someone planted a tree a long time ago."

The Maharaja planted the tree of humanity, and its shade still protects generations of Poles today. In recognition of his kindness, Poland posthumously honored him, and even today, the Polish people remember him as the man who gave them hope when the world had turned its back.

POLAND'S TRIBUTE TO THE MAHARAJA

Poland has never forgotten the Maharaja's kindness. In recognition of his humanitarian efforts, he was posthumously honored with:

1. Good Maharaja Square (SkwerDobregoMaharadzy) in Warsaw

2. The Commander's Cross of the Order of Merit by Poland

3. JamsahebDigvijaysinhJadeja School in Warsaw

4. A Parliamentary Resolution in Poland in 2016 commemorating his aid to Polish refugees

Here are a few ways you can start creating your own legacy:

1. **Live with Purpose**: Identify your core values and make sure your actions align with them. Every decision you make should reflect the person you want to be remembered as.

2. **Help Others**: One of the most powerful ways to leave a legacy is to help others discover and use their own gifts. Your

mentorship, guidance, and encouragement can have a ripple effect that lasts for generations.

3. **Be a Positive Influence**: Strive to be someone who lifts others up, spreads positivity, and makes the world a better place through small, everyday actions.

4. **Think Beyond Yourself**: Legacy isn't about you—it's about the lives you touch. Think

Legacy : Leaving the World a Better Place 95

about how you can make a lasting impact that will benefit others for years to come.

Your gift is not just for you—it's for the world. And when you use it with intention, you create a legacy that will live on long after you're gone. So, start today. Think about the legacy you want to leave and take action to ensure that your impact lasts beyond your lifetime.

❖ ❖ ❖

Chapter Thirteen

Conclusion: The World Needs Your Superpowers

As you turn the final page of this book, a new chapter in your life begins. Everything you've read, every story you've resonated with, every insight you've discovered, has led to this pivotal moment—the moment where you decide to take action. The lessons shared here are not meant to stay confined to the pages of this book; they are meant to be lived, embodied, and shared with the world.

As Paulo Coelho wisely wrote in The Alchemist, "When you want something, all the universe conspires in helping you to achieve it."

The moment you acknowledge your superpower and commit to using it, the world will align in unexpected ways to support your journey. Opportunities will present themselves, the right people will cross your path, and the strength you never knew you had will rise within you.

But remember—recognizing your gift is only the beginning. The true magic happens when you act on it, when you step forward despite uncertainty, and when you embrace the belief that you were meant for more. The world is waiting for your unique talents, your perspective, and your light. Don't let self-doubt or hesitation hold you back. The universe is ready to conspire in your favor, but it all starts with you taking that first step.

So go forth, embrace your power, and create the life you were always meant to live. The best is yet to come.

STEP INTO ACTION

The first and most important step in this journey is to recognize that you are ready. No more waiting for the perfect moment or the ideal circumstances. The journey to unlocking your unique potential begins now. Start where you are, with what you have. Each small step forward will build momentum, and before you know it, you'll look back and marvel at how far you've come.

Think about all the qualities and abilities you've unearthed while reading this book. Maybe you've realized you're a natural leader, a compassionate healer, an innovative thinker, or a bold dreamer. Whatever it is, acknowledge it. Write it down. Let this be your starting point.

PRACTICAL STEPS TO BEGIN YOUR JOURNEY

1. Set Clear Intentions: Start with clarity. What is the one thing you've always felt drawn to but hesitated to pursue? Define it. Whether it's a skill, a passion, or a calling, give it a name and let it become your north star.

2. Create a Vision Board: Visualize the life you want to lead and the person you aspire to become. Collect images, quotes, and symbols that represent your goals. Place it somewhere you can see daily as a constant reminder of your purpose.

3. Take Micro Steps: Grand transformations begin with small actions. If you dream of being a writer, start journaling. If leadership calls to you, take on small leadership roles. Focus on progress, not perfection.

4. Surround Yourself With the Right People: As discussed in earlier chapters, the company you keep shapes your journey. Seek out mentors, peers, and friends who uplift you, challenge you, and believe in your potential. Their positive energy will fuel your progress.

5. Embrace Failure as Growth: Fear of failure holds so many back from starting. Remember, each setback is a lesson, a stepping stone to greater success. Learn, adapt, and keep moving forward.

6. Practice Gratitude: Gratitude keeps your heart open and your mind focused on abundance. Celebrate every milestone, no matter how small, and be thankful for the opportunities that come your way.

THE WAVES OF CHANGE YOU CREATE

When you step into your power and live authentically, you don't just change your life—you inspire others. Your courage to take the road less travelled becomes a beacon for those around you, encouraging them to explore their own potential. Imagine the impact you could have: your small, consistent efforts could ripple outward, touching lives in ways you can't even imagine.

Think of the stories we've shared in this book—ordinary people who discovered extraordinary strength within themselves. You have the same potential. By stepping into your journey, you become the hero of your own story and a source of inspiration for others.

WRITE YOUR LEGACY

Your journey is uniquely yours, and so is the legacy you will leave behind. This is not about fame or accolades; it's about living a life that feels true to you. A life where you fully embrace your gifts, share them with the world, and make a difference, however big or small.

Take a moment to ask yourself: What do I want my legacy to be? How do I want to be remembered? Let these questions guide your decisions, actions, and priorities moving forward.

THE TIME IS NOW

As you close this book, remember that the greatest gift you can give yourself is to take that first step. You don't need all the answers, and you don't need to have it all figured out. Trust that the journey will unfold as you move forward, and each step will reveal the path ahead.

The world needs your unique abilities, your perspective, and your light. Don't let doubt or fear hold you back. You are capable of extraordinary things, and your journey begins now.

So take a deep breath, trust yourself, and step boldly into the life you were meant to lead. The best is yet to come.

❖ ❖ ❖

Final Words of Inspiration

You are a superhero. You have the power to change your life, to impact the lives of others, and to leave behind a legacy that will outlive you. The gifts you've carried with you throughout your life, often hidden or overlooked, are the key to unlocking the life you've always dreamed of. It's not too late to recognize your potential, no matter how old you are, no matter what stage of life you're in.

Life has a way of clouding our view of our own strengths. It can be easy to get caught up in the routines, the fears, and the doubts. But deep down, your superpowers have always been there, waiting to be awakened. Now, it's your time.

The world is waiting for your unique gifts. No one else can fulfill your purpose. There is no one else like you in the world, and that makes you invaluable. Whether you choose to use your abilities for your personal growth, to help others, or to change the world, know that your contribution matters. **Your superhero journey begins now.**

So, take that first step. You don't need to have all the answers, but you do need to take action. **Start today.**

The world needs what only you can offer.

❖ ❖ ❖

About The Author

Rishabh Agarwal is a seasoned corporate professional and a motivational voice, inspiring individuals through this book to unlock their hidden potential and embrace their unique superpowers. Born in the holy city of Prayagraj, Rishabh built his corporate career primarily in New Delhi, the national capital, and now resides in Baroda, India. His journey stands as an illustration of self-discovery and purpose-driven action.

Rishabh is an alumnus of **Indian Institute of Management (IIM) Calcutta, Indian Institute of Technology (IIT) Kanpur, and IIT Madras** where he pursued management education, and **HBTI Kanpur,** where he earned his engineering degree. His diverse academic background blends technical expertise with strategic leadership, shaping his approach to innovation and problem-solving.

He is **certified by the Japan International Cooperation Agency (JICA) under the International Cooperation Program of the Government of Japan** and was personally recognized by renowned management expert **Shoji Shiba, MIT (Massachusetts Institute of Technology | Sloan School of Management)** — for adaptive leadership and multicultural management during his Japan visit.

He has held leadership roles in globally renowned organizations, including Fluor Corporation, Air Products, Escorts Ltd., and Simon Carves, where he drove innovation in supply chain and operations. Currently, Rishabh serves as **Director at Xovian Aerospace Technologies**, an aerospace tech company, where he blends his strategic insight with a passion for advancing cutting-edge technology.

Rishabh's leadership and contributions were recognized at the **Indian Space Conclave**, where he received a prestigious award from the **Indian Space Research Organization (ISRO)** for excellence in the Space Services - Remote Sensing Segment, acknowledging his impact in the sector.

Beyond his corporate achievements, Rishabh is deeply engaged in academia and thought leadership. He is a **Board Member of the Institution's Innovation Council (IIC) at Jaipuria Institute of Management, Ghaziabad**, and has served as a **visiting faculty at CCS Meerut University**, sharing his expertise in supply chain, logistics, and innovation with aspiring leaders. A holder of the prestigious **Top One**

percentile score in CAT, he has also distinguished himself early on by winning several Maths and Science Olympiads.

His work has taken him across the globe, from the USA to China and Japan, giving him a wealth of diverse experiences that enrich his perspectives. He is also a sought-after speaker, at events like **ProCargo Connect** with his ability to connect, inspire, and empower.

In this book, Rishabh combines compelling stories, transformative lessons, and actionable insights to help readers discover the superhero within themselves. His writing speaks to the universal longing for purpose, guiding readers to rise above self-doubt, break free from limitations, and create a life of meaning and impact.

Rishabh is a lifelong learner, passionate about exploring the intersection of technology and human potential. He also enjoys mentoring aspiring leaders and fostering innovation through his work in aerospace, supply chain, and logistics.

This book is more than a guide—it's an invitation to rediscover your inner brilliance and step boldly into the life you were destined to lead.

Visit: www.rishabhagarwal.in for more insights, inspiration, and updates.

Made in the USA
Coppell, TX
12 April 2025